The Soldier

# THE WORLD WAR II SOLDIER AT MONTE CASSINO

By William R. Sanford and Carl R. Green

Illustrations by George Martin

Edited by Jean Eggenschwiler
and Kate Nelson

PUBLISHED BY

# Capstone Press

Mankato, MN, U.S.A.

**Distributed By**

**ϤP** CHILDRENS PRESS®
CHICAGO

# CIP

## LIBRARY OF CONGRESS CATALOGING IN PUBLICATION DATA

Sanford, William R. (William Reynolds), 1927-
The World War II soldier at Monte Cassino / by William R. Sanford, Carl
R. Green.--: edited by Jean Eggenschwiler and Kate Nelson.
  p. cm.-- (The Soldier)
Summary: Recreates the experiences of one soldier in World War II as he
fights in the battle of Monte Cassino.
**ISBN 1-56065-005-2**
1. Cassino (Italy), Battle of, 1944-- Juvenile literature. 2. Morimoto, Larry,
1920-- Juvenile literature. [1. Cassino (Italy), Battle of, 1944. 2. World
War, 1939-1945--Campaigns.] I. Green, Carl R. II. Eggenschwiler, Jean.
III. Nelson, Kate. IV. Title. V. Title: World War II soldier at Monte
Cassino. VI. Title: 1944-- the World War two soldier at Monte Cassino.
VII. Title: 1944--the World War 2 soldier at Monte Cassino. VIII. Series:
Sanford, William R. (William Reynolds), 1927- Soldier.
D763.I82C2666  1989
940.54'215622--dc20      **89-25187  CIP  AC**

## PHOTO CREDITS

Illustrated by George Martin
Designed by Nathan Y. Jarvis & Associates, Inc.

# Capstone Press

Box 669, Mankato, MN, U.S.A. 56001

# CONTENTS

# A NEW WORLD WAR
# BEGINS

The seeds of a new war were planted in the treaty that ended World War I. The victors, led by Britain and France, forced Germany to accept the blame for that war. With the blame came a huge bill for war damages. The proud Germans also had limits placed on the size of their armed forces.

President Woodrow Wilson of the United States knew the peace treaty was flawed. He put his hopes for the future in the **League of Nations**. But the League of Nations was crippled from the start. Despite Wilson's best efforts, the United States never joined. Congress would not accept the treaty. That was serious, but the flaw ran even deeper. When trouble broke out, the League could not force the warring nations to make peace.

A world **depression** struck in the 1930s. Millions of people lost their jobs. Widespread hunger and despair led to the rise of dictators in Italy and Germany. Military leaders gained control of Japan. After building strong armies the three nations set out to conquer their neighbors. History books say that World War II started when the Germans marched into Poland in 1939. But by then Japanese armies were already fighting in China.

Most Americans tried to ignore the war that was sweeping across Europe and Asia. They wanted the United States to steer clear of foreign conflicts. That feeling was made stronger by the Great Depression. Jobs were scarce. Nobody wanted to pay for a large and modern army. If war should come, people said, the nation's citizen-soldiers could be called to duty. That was a tradition that went back to the Revolutionary War.

Larry Morimoto was one of those citizen-soldiers. When he was 18, Larry joined the 299th Regiment of the Hawaiian Territorial Guard. The Guard trained on

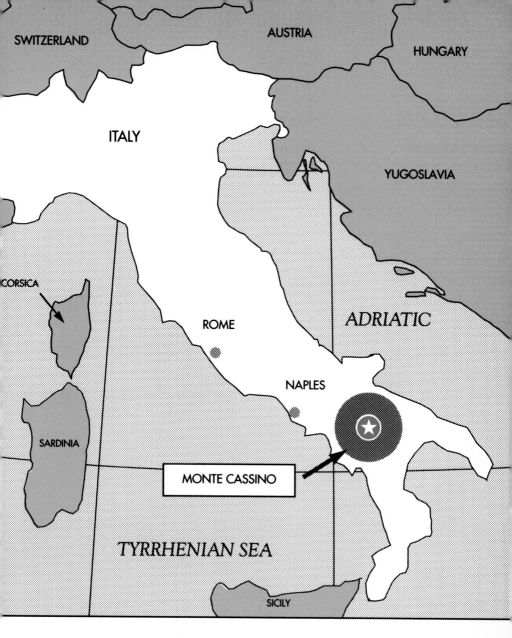

Monte Cassino, Italy, and the surrounding battle area.

weekends and during the summer. Larry did not want to go to war, but he enjoyed "playing soldier." Anything seemed better than working in his family's store on the big island of Hawaii. The two-week summer training camps on the island of Oahu were best, he thought.

In November of 1941, Larry turned 21. His parents gave him a trip to California as a present. Larry stayed with his aunt and uncle in Los Angeles. Uncle Hiro owned a small plant nursery. It was a great vacation. Larry took in all of the sights. Watching a movie being made was a special treat.

Even on vacation, Larry could not ignore the grim news that filled the newspapers. President Franklin Roosevelt told Japan to pull out of China. To back up the demand, oil sales to Japan were cut off. At the same time, young men were being called to serve in the armed forces. When people met on the street, they talked mostly about the chances of going to war.

Larry was still in Los Angeles on December 7, 1941. That was the day the Japanese bombed Pearl Harbor.

# THE RELOCATION CAMP

The Morimoto family huddled around the radio. A Los Angeles station was repeating the news of the disaster at Pearl Harbor.

Larry turned to his uncle. Like Larry's father, Uncle Hiro was an **Issei** [EES-say]. The Issei were immigrants from Japan who had settled in the U.S. Larry was a **Nisei** [NEE-say], a native American born to Japanese parents.

"It has to be a mistake," Larry said. "Why would the Japanese want to bomb Hawaii?"

Uncle Hiro chose his words with care. "Japan is run by military warlords," he said. "They led their country into a war with China that has dragged on for years. Now they want to conquer Southeast Asia. If they succeed, they will gain valuable oil and food supplies. They know that the U.S. Navy is the only force strong enough to stop them. The attack on Pearl Harbor was an attempt to cripple our fleet."

"But America is the strongest country in the world," Larry said. "Japan doesn't have a chance against us."

Hiro shook his head sadly. "Japan used a

U.S. Army Transportation Museum Photo

sneak attack to win a war once before. In 1905, they surprised and sank a Russian fleet. That victory led to a quick peace. The warlords are wrong, though, if they think we will give up easily."

Larry noticed that Hiro called the Japanese "they". The Americans were "we". He felt the same way. In Hawaii, his classmates had been of Filipino, Chinese, Japanese, Portuguese, Hawaiian, and mainland ancestry. They all thought of themselves as Americans.

On December 8 Larry tried to book passage back to Hawaii. The shipping agent told him that the armed forces had taken all the berths. "That's okay," Larry thought. "I'll work in a defense plant until I'm called to active duty."

A few nights later Hiro saw that Larry was too upset to eat. "What's the matter?" he asked.

"It's not fair!" Larry said bitterly. "I've been to all the aircraft plants. They won't let me apply for a job. One security officer told me, 'We don't want Jap spies in our factory!' Then he drew his pistol and marched me out the door."

Hiro patted his nephew on the back.

"Keep your chin up," he warned. "I'm afraid things will get worse."

The next few weeks proved that Hiro was right. Larry learned that the army was not going to call him to active service. All Japanese-Americans had been discharged from the Territorial Guard. Banks refused to cash his checks. His life insurance was cancelled. The Morimotos were also victims of the new hatred of anything Japanese. At school, Larry's cousins were beaten up. The milkman refused to make deliveries. Many florists stopped buying Hiro's flowers.

A heavier blow fell in February, 1942. President Roosevelt signed an order that set up military security districts. People thought to be disloyal could be forced to leave the districts. When the army posted the order its full impact became clear. All Japanese living on the West Coast would have to move out.

The Nisei argued that their civil rights were being denied. The army refused to listen. The commanding general snapped, "A Jap is a Jap! It makes no difference that he's an American." Hiro had to sell his home and business. Then, under armed guard, Larry and the Morimotos were taken to a train station. The station was filled with Japanese-

Americans. Their next stop was a **relocation camp** at Topaz, Utah.

A freezing desert wind greeted the Morimotos at Topaz. Their new home was a 20x25 foot room in a wooden **barracks**. The thin walls did not keep out the cold. With teeth chattering, Larry and Hiro shoveled dirt against the outside walls. That kept the wind from whistling through the cracks in the floor. Their only warmth came from a pot-bellied stove. The stove was also used for cooking.

Larry sent letters to the men in charge of the camp. "The Japanese-Americans in Hawaii are still free," he wrote. "Why am I here? I was only in Los Angeles for a visit. If you let me leave, I'll join the army." No one answered his letters.

The Morimotos found ways to stay busy. Aunt Mariko and her children took jobs making camouflage netting. They earned less than a dollar a day. Uncle Hiro planted a garden and took care of the camp's chickens. Larry taught math classes and wrote for the camp newspaper. His articles were censored before they were printed.

Each night, Larry crossed a day off his calendar. "I'm going crazy," he told Hiro. "I must get out of here."

# OUT OF THE CAMP AND
# INTO THE ARMY

The news Larry was hoping for came through in June of 1942. The army was changing its mind about the Japanese-Americans. A big reason was the work the former Territorial Guardsmen were doing in Hawaii. After being thrown out of the Guard, they formed the Varsity Victory Volunteers. Working without pay, they did clean-up and construction jobs on Hawaii's military bases. Their hard work proved their loyalty.

General Emmons said the army should form a special unit of Hawaiian-born Japanese-Americans. He wanted the unit to be trained on the mainland. If the Japanese hit Hawaii again, he reasoned, the Nisei might be mistaken for invaders. When the plan was approved, the Hawaiian Provisional Battalion began to sign up Nisei volunteers.

Larry's letter-writing paid off. A camp official told him he could enlist in the new unit. He said goodbye to his aunt and uncle and took a train to Oakland, California. That was where he joined the Provisional Battalion. Two days later, on June 12, the unit was renamed the 100th Infantry Battalion. The men called their outfit the "One Puka Puka" [poo-ka poo-ka]. That was island **pidgin** for "One Zero Zero." Pidgin was a mixture of Hawaiian, English and Japanese. It was useful when the men did not want outsiders to understand them.

Three trains carried the 100th to Camp McCoy in Wisconsin. The training course began at once. Larry drove himself to keep up with the fast pace. The unit marched and drilled through a summer of fierce heat. "You have to be in shape to kill Germans," the drill sergeant roared.

After one long session of push-ups, Larry flopped into the shade of a tree. He kept quiet when he heard two officers talking on the other side of the tree. He knew he was not doing anything wrong, but you never knew about officers. At times they seemed to delight in making life hard for privates.

"Finding uniforms for these little guys is tough," one voice complained. "They average 5'4", and they weigh 125 pounds soaking wet. Some of them wear size 4 shoes! I feel like I'm trying to outfit an army of Munchkins."

"The mess officers are going crazy, too," said the second voice. "Who ever heard of an army that eats rice three times a day? But I'll say this. These guys catch on quick and they never quit. They are more 'gung ho' than the Marines!"

After the officers left, Larry told his squad what he had heard. They looked pleased. "If Uncle Sam needs soldiers," Timmy Hacha said, "we're his boys."

Day by day, the training grew more intense. As a guardsman, Larry already knew how to do close-order drill. He could march, salute, and snap his rifle to "inspection arms" like a veteran. But that was kid stuff. They were combat soldiers now. Their lives depended on how well they mastered their new lessons.

Fall gave way to a cold winter. Larry was taught to fire carbines, machine guns,

and anti-tank weapons. He learned to use a gas mask and to throw a **grenade**. In the field, the men practiced patrolling, map reading, and digging in. Larry knew that a

**foxhole** might save his life when German **snipers** were shooting at him.

In February of 1943, it was time to begin advanced training. The 100th moved to Camp Shelby, Mississippi. The warm weather felt good to the Hawaiians after the cold northern winter. There was more good news waiting at Camp Shelby. The army was now enlisting all Japanese-Americans, not just those born in Hawaii. Three thousand Hawaiians and 1,500 mainland volunteers formed the 442nd Regimental Combat Team. Most of the officers were white Americans. The new unit arrived at Camp Shelby in May. It was almost three times bigger than the 100th.

The men from the 100th found old friends in the 442nd. Larry visited his cousin Toro in the 442nd's barracks. "Hey, Toro," he called. "What are you Katonks doing here?" "Katonk" was the Hawaiian name for a main-lander. It came from the sound an empty coconut makes when it hits the ground.

Toro looked up from the boots he was polishing. "Larry, you old Buddhahead," he said with a smile. That was the mainlander's version of the pidgin insult "buta-head." It meant "pighead."

The cousins compared shoulder patches. Larry's patch showed that he belonged to the 100th. It carried the motto, "Remember Pearl Harbor." Toro's 442nd patch showed an arm holding the torch of liberty. Soon they were swapping stories about their training. Both men said they were eager to see some action.

## "FIGHTING A WAR WILL SEEM EASY AFTER THIS"

"I've got mud in my hair and sand in my food," Larry sighed. "The war will seem like a picnic after Camp Shelby."

The drafty barracks reminded Larry of the relocation camp. After training all day, the men had to work at night to fix up the old buildings. Friday nights were the worst. Instead of relaxing, they had to clean everything for a Saturday inspection. Sometimes the barracks did not pass the captain's "white glove test." Then they had to clean it all over again.

The war games came almost as a relief. The One Puka Puka was assigned to the Blue team. After the Red team set up a defensive line the Blues were sent to attack it. That usually meant a long march through muddy swamps. Sometimes it rained, but the war games went on. The games taught Larry the sounds and smell and fatigue of battle.

"I've been spending a lot of time on my belly," Larry told Toro that weekend. "I wiggle under barbed wire and I crawl through swamp water. The only time I'm not on all fours is at chow time. After a day in the field, even **C-rations** taste good."

Toro made a face. "You can't be serious," he said. "I hope I never see canned meats and canned biscuits again." He slapped his neck. "But there's something worse than army food. I'm being eaten alive by mosquitos."

Larry felt better on the day his battalion commander called the unit together. "Men," he said, "you've scored top marks in these war games. Your success will make it easier for the other Japanese-Americans who follow you."

Larry earned a marksman's badge with his rifle, the .30 caliber **M-1**. The M-1 weighed 9.5 pounds and held an 8-shot clip. Unlike older rifles, the soldiers did not have to work a bolt action between shots. The gases released when the gun fired ejected the spent shell and cocked the hammer. Larry also drilled with a **bayonet** attached to his rifle. The knife-like blade turned the rifle into a vicious weapon for hand-to-hand combat.

The troops were trained to use many new weapons. Larry preferred the Browning light machine gun. The gun's high rate of fire gave it a strong knockout punch. "No one can stand up to 600 rounds a minute," he thought. Larry also fired an anti-tank weapon called the bazooka. The pipe-like weapon was loaded with rockets that took off with a "whoosh".

Holding a live hand grenade still made Larry nervous. "Are you sure this won't go off in my hand?" he asked Sergeant Tanaka.

The sergeant held up a grenade. "A grenade can't go off until you pull the pin and release the safety lever. Even then, you have 4.5 seconds before it explodes. These babies only weigh 1.3 pounds, so you can throw them quite a ways. Toss one into a German machine gun nest and KA-BOOM! No more **Jerries**!"

Larry saw that the hard training was welding the 100th into a team. It helped that the men came from Hawaii. Many were related. Others had been friends since childhood. Each man felt that doing less than his best would let the team down. Their officers told them that no other unit could match their spirit.

When they were off duty, the men joked a lot. Larry laughed hardest at his friends who were sent to a K-9 training center. The idea was to teach the K-9 dogs to pick up the scent of Japanese soldiers. The dogs tracked the men to their hiding places— and then licked their faces. Clearly, the animals knew that these "Japanese" were Americans.

Another story that ran through the camp was not a laughing matter. The rumor said that some officers were secretly questioning the 100th's loyalty. The men did not like the idea of being spied on. They knew they were good Americans.

Rumors or no rumors, training went on. Larry was learning the army's special language. His **GI** (government issue) uniform was OD (olive drab) in color. He took his turn at KP (kitchen police) and hated PT (physical training). Metal dogtags stamped with his name and army number hung around his neck.

A careful dresser at home, Larry did not like the looks of his combat uniform. In battle he would wear a flannel shirt, field jacket, baggy pants, and combat boots. He would also carry his rifle and ammo belt, rations, and a ground sheet to sleep on. A canteen and folding shovel completed the outfit.

"Sarge, this uniform is too big for me," Larry complained to the supply sergeant. "Even my boots are a size too big."

The wrinkled old soldier did not even smile. "Son," he said, "you're going out to kill Germans, not to dance with them."

# "WATCH OUT, HITLER, HERE WE COME!"

Larry received his corporal's stripes in August of 1943. He earned the promotion by being named the top soldier in his squad. The long training period had lasted over a year.

"I've peeled tons of potatoes and stood a hundred inspections," he wrote to his parents. "Every Saturday we spit-shine our boots and arrange our foot lockers. Then we line up next to our bunks for Captain Terry to inspect us. This morning, for the first time in a month, we passed! As a reward, we have the rest of the day off. Toro and I plan to go bowling at the camp PX (post exchange)."

The war news was getting better. The

U.S. and its allies had driven the Germans out of North Africa. In the Pacific, American forces had stopped the Japanese advance. "The 100th is ready to fight," Larry wrote. "I wish our orders would come through."

Larry's wish was granted on August 11. The 100th boarded a train and headed north. On all sides the men saw signs of a country at war. Highway speeds had been reduced to 35 mph to save gas. Billboards urged Americans to buy war bonds and to share rides. A colorful poster on the train advised, "Loose lips sink ships." It reminded the men that spies might be anywhere.

Larry's mother wrote from Hawaii to tell him about **rationing**. Each week an adult was allowed 28 ounces of meat, 4 ounces of butter, and 8 ounces of sugar. His father was limited to 3 gallons of gas a week for pleasure driving. Cigarettes, candy, and liquor were scarce. Larry's sister missed nylon stockings the most. The air force needed nylon for parachutes.

After a few days at a camp in New Jersey the 100th was trucked to Brooklyn. Waiting at the pier was a former banana boat, the *James Parker*. The troopship's cargo hold had been turned into a sleeping compartment. The bunks were stacked three high and the portholes were sealed. Larry was carrying his rifle and a full pack when he walked up the gangplank.

On August 21, 1943 the ship steamed out of New York harbor. It soon fell into place in a convoy. Sleek destroyers circled the slow-moving troopships and freighters. The need for warships became all too clear on the third day out. Larry was leaning on the rail when a lookout yelled, "Periscope!"

A typical bunk arrangement on a troop transport ship.

The destroyers raced in to drop depth charges. The men cheered when the captain announced that a German U-boat had been sunk.

Half of the men were seasick, even though the Atlantic was calm. The rest played the game of guessing where they would see action. The North African campaign had ended in May. Mussolini, Italy's dictator, had quit in July. The island of Sicily had fallen on August 17. Larry studied a map of Europe. It looked as though Italy would be the next stop for the Allied armies.

Shipboard life soon settled into a routine. Larry stood in one line to eat and waited in another to take a shower. There was even a line to see the nightly movie. With so many sick soldiers below decks, he spent as much time on deck as he could. The lifeboat drills were welcome breaks in the long days.

At last the ship steamed past the Rock of Gibralter. After 12 days at sea, the 100th landed in Algeria, North Africa. On September 3 exciting news reached the camp. "The British 8th Army has landed at the tip of Italy," Sergeant Takata told the squad.

"That's too far south," Larry said. "I bet the real landings will come farther north, towards Naples."

The next news was less exciting. The army was assigning the 100th to guard North African supply trains. "We didn't join up to be train conductors," Larry told Sergeant Takata. This time the old soldier could only shrug. He was angry, too.

Colonel Farrant Turner, the commander of the 100th, agreed with his men. He went to General Mark Clark, who commanded the 5th Army. "Asking the 100th to guard trains is a waste of a trained combat division," Turner argued. Clark responded by attaching the 100th to the 34th "Red Bull" Division. The men of the 34th were veterans of the fighting in North Africa.

The war in Italy changed almost daily. On September 8 the Italians surrendered. On the next day the 5th Army invaded Italy at Salerno, 30 miles below Naples. The Germans fought back, even though their Italian allies had given up.

On September 19 Larry boarded ship again. The 34th Division was on its way to Salerno. "Watch out Hitler!" Larry yelled. "The 100th is on its way!"

# THE ROAD TO MONTE CASSINO

The 100th landed at Salerno in late September. The wreckage left by the battle for the beachhead two weeks earlier lay all around them. The men cursed the heavy rain that fell that night. Sergeant Takata told them they would change their tune when the cold weather came. "Rain is better than snow and sleet," he said.

On September 26 trucks carried the 100th 20 miles inland to the front lines. For the first time, they were within radio range of the enemy. The Hawaiian walkie-talkie operators switched to pidgin. Larry smiled when he heard them. It must drive the Germans crazy to hear, "Hama hama Tommy gun boltsu, hayaku eh, and ammo mote kite kudasi," he thought. The message meant,

"Rush order. Send a machine gun bolt and more ammunition."

The 100th had its first taste of combat on September 29. Baker Company's Lieutenant Froming and Sergeant Takata led the way. Larry was close behind them. The Germans opened fire with machine guns and mortars when the men rounded a bend in the road. As the company took cover, Takata spotted a machine gun nest. He raced towards it, firing his Tommy gun as he ran. Larry was stunned to see Takata fall with a German bullet in his head. The Sergeant was the 100th's first KIA (killed in action).

Covered by fire from his squad, Larry crawled close to the German gunners. Then he rolled on his side and lobbed a grenade into the nest. The explosion killed two Germans and silenced the gun. "That was for Sergeant Takata," Larry whispered.

The 100th was soon driving forward against stiff German resistance. The unit bypassed a village and hit a German artillery post near Montefalcione. Later, Larry led a patrol into the wrecked town. The Germans were nowhere to be seen.

In early October, the 100th was pulled back for a rest. Larry had lost track of time

while he was at the front. Each day seemed to last a year. He learned to eat and sleep whenever he had the chance. Death was a constant companion.

Larry's mood went up and down with the war news. The good news was that the

Allies had taken the port city of Naples. Their front line now stretched 80 miles across the width of Italy. The bad news was that the Germans were building strong defenses between Naples and Rome. General Kesselring was not going to retreat north without putting up a fight. The rugged Italian hills made his job easier. If they lost one hill, the Germans simply moved back to the next one.

On October 18 the 100th fought its way across the Volturno River. The men were learning to avoid the mines planted by the Germans. The worst, Larry decided, were the "bouncing Betties." These mines jumped three feet in the air before they exploded. The "screaming meemies" also got on Larry's nerves. The sound of those rockets, fired from six-barreled launchers, sent shivers down his spine.

Slowly the 100th pushed forward. A German armored regiment tried to stop them but failed. Then the Allied advance stopped. The Germans had settled into their Winter Line behind the Rapido River. The Allied foot soldiers would have to dig them out.

In November and December the 100th spent two weeks out of four at the front.

During their rest periods they caught up on sleep and stocked up on ammo. Hot meals made up for the cold **K-rations** they ate at the front. Larry met soldiers from Canada, New Zealand, France, India, Algeria, Morocco, and Poland. Many countries were fighting on the Allied side.

The cold weather was the enemy's ally. The U.S. army had not issued winter clothing. Larry's hands and feet often felt like lumps of ice. The medics warned the men to put on clean, dry socks whenever they could. That was the best way to avoid a painful case of **trench foot**.

Larry often went without sleep as the 100th stormed hill after hill. The victories were costly. Charlie (C) Company had only 50 men left out of 187. Easy (E) and Fox (F) Companies had been shot to pieces. Reporters were calling the 100th the "Purple Heart Battalion." The Nisei were winning hundreds of the medals given to men wounded in combat.

Toro Sakai was one of the 500 replacements who joined the 100th from the 442nd. Toro hugged Larry when the two men met in the rest area. "What's going to happen next?" Toro asked.

Larry knew that Toro was asking about the coming battle. "We have two tough nuts to crack. One is the Rapido River line and the other is Monte Cassino," he explained. "After that we'll be free to move straight up the Liri valley to Rome. But Captain Terry says he read about Monte Cassino in a textbook. It's one of the strongest defensive positions in the world."

# THE BATTLE OF MONTE CASSINO

Larry sipped a cup of hot coffee and huddled close to a mess tent stove. The 100th was resting after two weeks of combat. They had been fighting in the hills north of Monte Cassino.

"The British have crossed the Garigliano River near the Mediterranean," Timmy Hacha said. Timmy always seemed to know what was going on. "If they break through along the coast, they'll bypass Cassino. Then the Germans will have to retreat."

Sergeant Moto spoke up. "Sure, the British made it across the river. But then the Germans stopped them dead in their tracks," he said. "That's not all. Our 36th Division was cut to ribbons when it tried to cross the

Rapido River. Sorry, boys. We have to hit Monte Cassino head on."

On January 24, 1944 the 100th was back on the line. Larry looked across the open ground leading to the Rapido. He saw knee-deep mud and mine fields. Even if they made it through the mine fields, the swift, cold river still lay ahead. And the Germans were dug in on the far bank.

That night two companies dashed forward under an artillery **barrage**. Larry was one of the men detailed to drag rubber boats behind them. The soldiers were pinned down by heavy German fire before they reached the river. They had to take shelter behind a wall. Larry crouched there, breathing hard. As he watched, some officers blundered into a mine field. A "bouncing Betty" went off. It killed one man and wounded the unit commander.

A third company moved up to reinforce the two by the river. The 187 men were shielded by a smokescreen, but the German fire was heavy and accurate. Only 14 men made it to the wall. After that failure the survivors were pulled back to a reserve area.

While the unit regrouped, Timmy Hacha brought more news. "Our guys have landed at Anzio, 50 miles behind the German lines," he said. "They caught Kesselring by surprise. If nothing goes wrong, Rome will fall any day now."

But something did go wrong. The Americans at Anzio moved too slowly. Kesselring had time to bring in fresh troops. Once again the Allied drive was stalled.

The 100th was in reserve when the 34th Division fought its way across the Rapido. That was late in January. From a line north of Monte Cassino the attack turned southward. The advancing troops followed the mountain valleys. Early in February, the 100th rejoined the fighting. The fortress of Monte Cassino lay directly in their path.

From his shelter in a pile of rocks, Larry studied their target. The town of Cassino lay at the foot of a rugged mountain. An ancient stone **abbey** stood at its crest. The briefings had been clear. The Germans had fortified every ridge. Every path was planted with mines. Monte Cassino was truly a fortress.

The 100th fought its way into the northern outskirts of the town. In four days they advanced only 100 yards. The Germans had turned each stone house into a small fort. Before they could take a house, the GIs had to blast a hole in one wall. Then they rushed the house and cleaned it out, room by room.

On February 8 the 100th stormed Hill 165 (named for its height in meters). The generals wanted the hill because it guarded the easiest approach to the mountain. Resistance was light, and the unit moved quickly to the top. Larry's joy at the easy victory died quickly. He saw that the units on each side of the 100th were pinned down. "That's the heaviest fire I've ever seen," Larry muttered to Sergeant Moto. "The Jerries have us covered by machine guns, mortars, and artillery."

The 100th held Hill 165 for four days. Then, with the advance stalled, they were called back. The unit had lost 40 percent of its men in three weeks. After all the hard fighting, the Germans still owned Monte Cassino.

On February 15 Larry watched as the air force joined the battle. Wave after wave of bombers dropped two million pounds of bombs on Monte Cassino. Nearly 750 big guns added their shells to the bombardment. Huge clouds of smoke and dust rose high into the air. When the smoke cleared, both the town and the abbey had been turned to rubble.

"I bet no one survived that pounding," Toro told Larry.

Toro was wrong. Because of a mix-up in orders the American ground troops did not attack until the next day. By then the Germans had climbed out of their tunnels

and steel two-man shelters. Working quickly, they set up strong positions in the ruined buildings.

The 100th attacked Cassino for the last time on February 18. German gunners opened fire as Larry led his platoon forward. He was halfway up the mountain when his leg buckled. Looking down, Larry saw blood soaking through his pants. Two machine gun bullets had punched holes in his thigh. At the moment he did not feel any pain. That would come later, he knew.

A medic hustled up and sprinkled **sulfa powder** into the wound. Then he slapped on a pressure bandage to stop the bleeding. Larry tried to limp back to the fighting, but the leg would not support him. Two stretcher bearers carried him to an aid station. By then the unit was pulling back. The Germans still held the heights.

# AFTER THE BATTLE

The war ended for Larry on the slopes of Monte Cassino. The two lead slugs had shattered the bone in his thigh. The battle for Monte Cassino did not end for another four months. On May 18, 1944 a Polish corps finally captured the abbey atop Monte Cassino.

The 100th still had some hard fighting to do. In late March the One Puka Puka landed at the Anzio beachhead near Rome. In early June the men rolled through Rome. There they heard that the Allies had landed in France. For the first time since Camp Shelby the 100th was joined by the 442nd. Together, the two units advanced northward.

From Italy the 100th was sent to southern France. Soon it was fighting along the French-German border. By the spring of 1945 the unit was back in Italy. The men were moving up the Po Valley on May 8 when the Germans gave up. The war in the Pacific ended four months later.

The men of the 100th and the 442nd counted their losses. They had paid a high price to prove their loyalty. The units had 680 men KIA and earned 9,486 Purple Hearts. Among their 18,000 medals were a Congressional Medal of Honor and 52 Distinguished Service Crosses. As General Joseph Stilwell said, "The Nisei bought an awful big hunk of America with their blood."

Larry was still in a veterans hospital when the war ended. After his leg mended, he had to learn to walk again. At last, in November of 1945 he returned to Hawaii. His family put on a huge luau to celebrate his return. After the feast his father asked Larry about his plans.

"I want to go to college to study agriculture," Larry said. "My benefits from the GI Bill will help put me through the University of Hawaii. After I graduate, I'll go into the flower business with Uncle Hiro. He will help me buy some land on the slopes of Mount Haleakala on Maui."

In 1952 Larry shipped his first load of proteas to the mainland. The exotic flowers were a great success. Two years later he married his childhood sweetheart, Susie Kato. Together they built a house near the ocean. The war seems far away these days, except when storm clouds build up over Maui. Larry knows when the storm is close. That's when the old wound in his thigh begins to ache.

# GLOSSARY

### Important Historic Figures

**GENERAL MARK CLARK** (1896-1984)—The commanding officer of the American forces at the Battle of Monte Cassino.

**ADOLPH HITLER** (1889-1945)—German dictator whose attempt to dominate Europe was a direct cause of World War II.

**GENERAL ALBERT KESSELRING** (1887-1960)— German general who commanded the German forces defending Monte Cassino.

**PRESIDENT FRANKLIN ROOSEVELT** (1882-1945)— 32nd President of the United States. Roosevelt led the nation during most of World War II, but died in office before the war ended.

### Important Terms

**ABBEY**—A church building where monks live and worship. The abbey at Monte Cassino was one of the largest in Europe.

45

**BARRACKS**—A building (or buildings) used to house soldiers.

**BARRAGE**—A heavy, sustained volume of artillery fire.

**BAYONET**—A long, sharp knife that attaches to the muzzle of a rifle. Soldiers use bayonets in hand-to-hand combat.

**C-RATIONS**—Canned foods that can be prepared quickly for troops in the field.

**DEPRESSION**—A period of severe economic troubles marked by a loss of jobs and lower business activity.

**FOXHOLE**—A shallow hole dug by a soldier as a way of avoiding enemy fire.

**GI**—A slang term for an American soldier during World War II. GI stands for "government issue," a term applied to anything provided by the army supply department.

**GRENADE**—A small bomb meant to be thrown by hand or fired from a specially equipped rifle.

**ISSEI**—An immigrant to the U.S. who was born in Japan.

**JERRY**—GI slang for German soldiers during World War II.

**K-RATIONS**—High-calorie packaged foods that soldiers ate when they were in combat.

**LEAGUE OF NATIONS**—The forerunner of the United Nations. The League of Nations was formed after World War I, but wasn't strong enough to keep the peace.

**M-1 RIFLE**—The standard infantry weapon of World War II. The M-1 was a .30-caliber rifle that held an 8-shot clip.

**NISEI**—An American whose parents are Issei (Japanese immigrants).

**PIDGIN**—A simplified mixture of several languages.

**RATIONING**—The process of sharing goods that are in short supply. Rationing insures that everyone receives a fair share.

**RELOCATION CAMPS**—Isolated prisons in which many Japanese-Americans were held during World War II. The government took this action because it feared (wrongly) that the Issei and Nisei would spy for Japan.

**SNIPER**—A sharpshooter who fires from a concealed position.

**SULFA POWDER**—A drug that prevents infection when it is sprinkled into a wound.

**TRENCH FOOT**—A painful foot disorder. A soldier gets trench foot when his feet are cold and wet for long periods of time.